AUTUMN PELTIER
CANADA

XIUHTEZCATL MARTINEZ
UNITED STATES

MAANASA MENDU
UNITED STATES

ARTEMISA XAKRIABÁ
BRAZIL

No WORLD TOO BiG

Young People Fighting Global Climate Change

Edited by **LINDSAY H. METCALF,**
KEILA V. DAWSON, *and* **JEANETTE BRADLEY**

Illustrated by **JEANETTE BRADLEY**

ini **Charlesbridge**

ON CLIMATE CHANGE

A found poem from the "Paris Agreement" by **Lindsay H. Metcalf**

Guided by
the need for
a just transition,
humankind
should   respect
the rights of
Mother Earth.

Individually, and together
strive to
long-term   mindful   action.

Global   resilience
is a   challenge   with
international dimensions.

Protect
ecosystems,
sharing
lessons learned.

Take the lead,
mobilizing   beyond
the   small.

The vision:
reduce greenhouse gas emissions.

Action
builds upon
burden.

Clear   the   gaps   with
equity
and the best available science.

The outcome:
nature   shall
provide,
its wish
fulfilled.

Nearly all of the world's countries signed the United Nations "Paris Agreement" in 2015, promising to reach climate neutrality—no increase in the greenhouse effect—by 2050. To achieve that goal we need to move away from burning fossil fuels, which produce heat-trapping gases that blanket the earth. Young people are watching, questioning, and demanding that world leaders keep their promise. Meet a few young activists who are working to secure the future of the planet we share.

ZANAGEE ARTIS: WE ARE ZERO HOUR

A sea chantey by **Jeanette Bradley**

At first at school it was just me—
calling for recycled paper.
We need change now, why can't you see?
It's already zero hour.

And they nodded and smiled and all agreed,
but nothing ever happened.
I remembered how my moms taught me:
we need to work together.

We're at zero hour!
It's already zero hour!

Real change began once friends joined in—
raised seven hundred dollars.
Bottle refill station to begin—
the group could make things happen.

The summer before my senior year,
I met three young changemakers.
To fight Big Oil we'll start right here—
adults aren't acting for us.

We're at zero hour!
We'll call it Zero Hour!

With friends across the whole country,
we organized all year.
We marched through Washington, DC,
chanting *This is Zero Hour!*

So many things I want to be,
though our future is uncertain.
But I have hope, and it grows when we
come together as Zero Hour.

Clinton, Connecticut, USA

Zanagee Artis tried to convince his school to ban plastic water bottles but wasn't successful until he started a school sustainability club. In 2017 Zanagee teamed up with fellow teens Jamie Margolin, Nadia Nazar, and Madelaine Tew to form Zero Hour. The next year they staged the first youth-led climate march in Washington, DC, with sister marches around the world. Zanagee's belief that young people will win against climate change is fueled by seeing his mothers succeed in their long fight for marriage equality.

MATE ACTION NOW

Start a climate club! Work together toward a small goal, then build on your success.

GRETA THUNBERG: ONE GIRL

A free verse poem by Sally J. Pla

One girl
found it scary-strange
that billions of grown-ups couldn't bear
to mention climate change
while oceans rose and forests burned.

She researched and learned
that the science was crystal clear.
And she flared with anger
at those grown-ups,
and she burned with fear.
How dare they harm our fragile world?

But what could *she* do—
one girl?

She inked a sign:
School Strike for Climate.
Bravely,
alone,
she stood on the Parliament steps
of stone.

But she wasn't alone for long.

One
grew to two
grew to hundreds,

until millions were standing strong
with
one
brave
girl.

Stockholm, Sweden

When Greta Thunberg learned about the greenhouse effect, she became sick with worry. Sometimes she couldn't talk or eat—until she turned her anxiety into action. Instead of starting ninth grade, Greta biked to the Swedish government building. This autistic teen's three-week protest demanded international action and inspired millions to stage weekly "Fridays for Future" climate protests around the world.

Think like an Earth protector. What are some ways you can live with less to help the planet?

XIUHTEZCATL MARTINEZ: A TURQUOISE MIRROR OF THE EARTH

A dokugin renga by **David Bowles**

His heart rooted deep
in ancestral tradition,
Xiuhtezcatl stands proud.

As a child he learns teotl
links living things in one web.

And that sacred spark
glows in him, too—whispering.
He must be its voice.

From the age of six he fights
to protect nature's balance.

His message rings clear
whether he speaks, raps, or writes:
we must be stewards.

Let's halt harmful practices
that hurt the environment.

Moved, judges listen,
and the people agree that
his name reflects truth—
he is a "turquoise mirror"
of our precious blue-green Earth.

Boulder, Colorado, USA

Xiuhtezcatl Martinez learned about teotl, the interconnectedness of humans and the earth, from his Indigenous Mexica culture. When he rapped a school presentation about climate change, he realized music could inspire others to speak for the planet. At fourteen he and his siblings released the eco hip-hop album *Generation Ryse*. Xiuhtezcatl was the youth director of the global organization Earth Guardians. He sued the government in multiple climate lawsuits and speaks tirelessly for climate justice.

Share a song, dance, or drawing to raise climate awareness and challenge the world to stop using fossil fuels.

THE MARSHALLESE YOUTH: iAKWE

A definition poem by **Carlon Zackhras**

ia·kwe

[yah-kweh] *noun*

Meaning:
hi, bye, love, and
you are as beautiful
as a rainbow.

We, the people
of the Marshall Islands,
have *iakwe*
for the fish in our seas
and the coconuts on our trees.

We have *iakwe*
for our songs sung in harmony
and our children splashing
in the blue.

Marshallese legend says
the ocean is made of drops.
You take care of your drop,
and I take care of mine.

When the wind blows
and the waves grow,
we little drops
can take care of the world

because

climate change will not destroy
our voices,
our hope,
our positivity,
our *iakwe.*

Marshall Islands

Young people in the Republic of the Marshall Islands created a Youth Leadership Coalition to learn how to advocate for worldwide climate progress. Teen poets and speakers, including Carlon Zackhras and Selina Leem, testified at United Nations climate change summits and explained the Marshall Islands' National Adaptation Plan for rising sea levels. The government is considering elevating their islands or building artificial islands so citizens can stay in the Pacific, protect Marshallese culture, and continue governing themselves.

SAVE OUR ISLANDS

Climate change is not your fault, but you can still speak up for your future.

ARTEMISA XAKRIABÁ: PROTECTOR AND ADVOCATE

An acrostic poem by Traci Sorell

Although she's young,

Rest assured,

Those in power know the

Emboldened

Mother Earth protector,

Indigenous climate activist, and

Student named

Artemisa

Xakriabá.

Advocating for her tribe and for

Key

Rights of

Indigenous peoples worldwide,

Artemisa

Believes we are

Áll responsible for our common home.

Xakriabá Indigenous Land, Minas Gerais, Brazil
Artemisa Barbosa Ribeiro, who also goes by Artemisa Xakriabá, was seven when she began planting trees to help reforest the Xakriabá people's lands in Brazil. She marches and sings to protest the burning of the Amazon rain forest and the killing of Indigenous protectors of our waters and forests. In 2019 she brought her message to the US Congress and the climate strike in New York City. Artemisa proclaims that the future of the planet and of Indigenous peoples are one and the same.

Organize a walk or bike event to raise money for an international environmental group that protects tropical rain forests.

LEAH NAMUGERWA: GROW

A dansa poem by JaNay Brown-Wood

The change you sow will grow
like the sapling of a tree
or the volume of a plea
when you spurn the status quo.
The change you sow will grow.

Bending down to hand and knee,
Leah plants tree after tree.
Though there's hundreds more to go,
the change one sows will grow.

Some adults may disagree,
but she knows she holds the key.
They won't dim her future's glow!
The change she sows will grow.

What a triumph it will be
when she plants that millionth tree.
And the youth who watch will know:
the change you sow will grow.

Kampala, Uganda

A landslide in the city of Kampala brought climate change home for Leah Namugerwa. Inspired by Fridays for Future, Leah began a strike in her school and was joined by fellow students. When Leah turned fifteen she planted two hundred trees. Her Birthday Trees project now provides thousands of saplings each year for others to plant. Leah rose to lead Fridays for Future Uganda, working with youth worldwide and calling for her country to ban plastic bags.

Celebrate your birthday by planting a tree. Gather your friends and have a tree-planting party!

MARINEL UBALDO: *I AM MARINEL*

A dramatic monologue by **Renée M. LaTulippe**

When the typhoon hit
our seaside village,
pummeled us to our knees,
it opened my eyes
wider than I wanted them
to be.

When the typhoon hit,
I saw a mother fall down with her child
and rise up with empty arms.

That is why
I
rise up now,
eyes wide open,
arms full of action.

Why
we must hold this world in our arms,
carry it gently
to next generations.

Why
I
raise my voice.

We are coming
with our typhoon
of climate knowledge.

We speak it.
We act it.
We sing it.
We dance it.

We bring it
so you will know

how to whip up the winds
of justice
and thunder your voice
for change.

Matarinao, Eastern Samar, Philippines

When Marinel Ubaldo was sixteen, a massive storm destroyed her village in the Philippines, killing thousands and depriving her family of food, water, and shelter. Marinel learned that warming oceans fuel more intense storms, threatening millions of people in coastal communities. She held theater productions to teach about climate change and attended the United Nations Climate Change Conference. Her activism spurred the Philippine government to hold big climate polluters accountable.

THIS IS my LiFe

Stage a play about the effects of climate change. Offer action steps the audience can take.

AUTUMN PELTIER: RENEWAL SEASON

A free verse poem by Aka Niviâna

Even though the bad things in the world
make it seem like eternal dark winter,
as if the light will not be seen again—
no matter what, my friend, I promise
light always returns,
warming up not only our bodies,
but our hearts.

Spring makes new flowers blossom inside us.
We feel it tingling from head to toe.

Summer carries us through life with an ease
we tend to forget is possible.

Soon comes Autumn, preparing us for another winter—
water-protecting, smile-infecting, hope-giving,
making you want to do good things for the world;
making you want to plant the hardy seed of joy
in the hearts of everyone.

Manitoulin Island, Ontario, Canada

Autumn Peltier grew up on Manitoulin Island surrounded by the deep waters of Lake Huron. When she was eight she visited another First Nations community and was shocked to find signs warning people not to drink or touch the tap water. She spoke out about the right to clean water and humans' responsibility to protect it from drought and pollution. When Autumn was fourteen she became the chief water commissioner of the Anishinabek Nation.

Be a water protector. Runoff from your yard or street drains into local waterways. Learn about pollutants to avoid at home.

LINA YASSIN: A BRIDGE TO THE FUTURE

A free verse poem by **Dalia Elhassan**

They want to sit in every pool, our blue earth says,
given a name in every language,
seven names for a single color,
a body broken by land.

I want to swim
in the pool of my own skin,
expand the volume of this body
beyond its capacity.

I am more than a vessel.
I am the bridge between
Arabic and English,
drought and flood,
past and future.

I craft newness from what remains,
cast the ashes of our collective mistakes
into any sea & watch the tide
return silver linings to my feet.

Khartoum, Sudan

Lina Yassin realized climate change was affecting Sudan when she volunteered to help Khartoum flood victims in 2013. No one was talking about climate change, so she wrote about it for her high-school newspaper. As a journalist writing in English and Arabic, Lina connects global climate change to local farming and food insecurity that forces people to migrate. She wrote, "We had the first climate war in history, which was the war in Darfur."

Research how climate change affects your community. Then write a letter to the editor of your local newspaper.

MAYA PENN: MAGIC TRASH

A free verse poem by **Vanessa Brantley-Newton**

Beauty is ageless

and can be created from
broken bits and pieces
of the past—

from vintage and discarded trash
recycled and upcycled by
a newfound creator
named Maya,
who set the fashion world
on fiyah with reimagined
jewelry and clothing that bring
life and beauty to bodies
of a new generation.

New chokers that choke out
the shame of chains
and pain,
giving new life
and beauty from ashes—
elements placed to the side
that become magic.

These fresh new ornaments,
to be laid upon
young and mature bodies,
were fashioned
by a brown girl's
hands at eight,
making something great
out of nothing—
making others feel
something like . . .
soul, grit, swag, grace,
and beauty.

Atlanta, Georgia, USA

Maya Penn created her own line of upcycled clothing when she was eight, proving that used clothes can be fashionable and fun. At eleven she expanded her company into a nonprofit called Maya's Ideas 4 the Planet. She designed and created eco-friendly, washable sanitary pads for girls in developing countries such as Senegal and Somalia. Maya's book, *You Got This!*, encourages young people to find their passion and make the world a better place.

Hand-me-downs help the earth! Swap clothes with friends or upcycle fashion from resale shops.

NIKITA SHULGA AND SOFiiA-KHRYSTYNA BORYSiUK: A RECiPE FOR EARTH

A projective verse by Lindsay H. Metcalf

When a landfill flamed
past capacity, a malady
      of glass, plastic,
    and food scraps
smothered sidewalks
in Lviv, Ukraine.
No one asked for
trash stew—
whoo! But what
could youth do?
Hours east in Kyiv,
Nikita knew that buried
food, boxed in from oxygen,
decayed into methane,
a climate-change cousin
twenty times stronger
than carbon dioxide.
Alongside Nikita,
Sofiia-Khrystyna
scraped plates, saving
waste with a taste for greatness.

These soilmates re*fused*
refuse in recipes of threes:
2 parts brown, 1 part green.
2 parts kid, 1 part grit.
They pleaded with school
leaders to believe in worms
whose squirms churned carbon
and nitrogen, the vitamins that
plants drink in. Bake at sunny-day
degrees for delicious weeks—
        rotting,
    watering,
  w *ri gg l i n g*
into fine flora food.
Their campaign trained
schools across Ukraine
    to serve a rich
    new menu:
    renewable,
      beautiful
        earth.

Kyiv, Ukraine

Nikita Shulga and Sofiia-Khrystyna Borysiuk were eleven when they heard about overflowing landfills in parts of Ukraine. They raised money and convinced a few schools in Kyiv to install compost bins, then fed cafeteria scraps to worms, which made fertile soil for plants. With support from Ukraine's ministers for ecology and education, their Compola project helped install more than 230 school composters. In their last year of high school, war with Russia disrupted the project and changed their lives.

Make your own compost! Diverting food waste from landfills keeps it from becoming methane, a powerful heat-trapping gas.

THE GREEN SCHOOL: BALI'S BIO BUS

A lục bát poem by **Teresa Robeson**

Cars, like ants, swarm to school.
Kids inside, keeping cool. No space
to park in a tight place—
auto fumes in your face … so loud …
bumper-to-bumper crowd—
enveloped by a cloud of smog.
It's one big eco-clog.

Kids had a dialogue: Go green!
Imagine the air clean.
Break free from gasoline. Why not
try cooking oil? We've got
lots from chefs, piping hot. Refit
buses so they emit
less carbon. Bit by bit, folks start
to change, to do their part:
Take the bus—it's just smart. Let's ride!

Bali, Indonesia

Students needed an idea for their 2015 senior service project at the Green School on the island of Bali. Because gasoline-fueled cars produce carbon dioxide, four students—Adam Handoko, Fabienne Koens, Cazmir Leenheer, and Kadek Rai—thought of a climate-friendly way to shuttle students to school. The seniors bought a bus and learned to make biodiesel from used cooking oil. Patrols of student "Grease Police" collected the oil across the island. After the first bio bus succeeded, other students converted more buses to create a fleet of green transportation.

Start a petition to ask your school district to switch to biodiesel or electric buses.

MAANASA MENDU: *THE POWER OF MOTION*

A free verse poem by Rajani LaRocca

Maanasa—
whose name means *mind*—
visited family in rural India,
saw the darkness
experienced by 1.2 billion,
wanted to make a difference.
So she tried and failed
and tried again.
As branches swayed in the wind,
she dreamed up
solar leaves
on piezoelectric stems:
her own HARVEST
that could power
rural and urban alike,
renewably.
Her bright example shows
we can try,
we can solve
global problems
together.
Like leaves,
we can move with the wind,
we can soak up the sun,
we can grow,
we can shine.

Mason, Ohio, USA

On family trips to India, eleven-year-old Maanasa Mendu noticed electricity blackouts and children studying by kerosene lamplight. How could she help? She knew about the piezoelectric effect, which produces electricity from movement. So she built an artificial leaf, attached it to a tree, and captured energy from the wind. Maanasa's five-dollar invention, HARVEST, produces electricity from three renewable sources—wind, sunlight, and rain. At thirteen, Maanasa was named America's Top Young Scientist.

Enter a science fair. What climate-change problem will you tackle?

MACKINTOSH ACADEMY: CAPTURE THE SUN

A free verse poem by Heidi E. Y. Stemple

"Keen minds. Compassionate hearts. Global action."
—*Mackintosh Academy motto*

Reach for the moon,
the students were told,
and even though they were
twelve years old,
these sixth-graders
would not be daunted.
They knew exactly
what they wanted.

Minds keen—calculated.
Hearts compassionate—evaluated.
Global action—activated.

Bring the power of the sun—
capture it to make things run.

From the idea
that students planted,
Mackintosh was proudly granted
          the sun in all its glory.

The moral of this solar story?

When "shoot for the moon" is your directive,
don't think it is your sole objective.
To the moon or pass it by—
there are no limits
          in your sky.

Littleton, Colorado, USA

Sixth-grade students at Mackintosh Academy in Littleton, Colorado, reached for the sky in 2014 to reduce the school's climate footprint. Skyler Bernard, Nicholas Booth, Sydney Gelman, Delia Guilbert, Aria Marizza, and Allie O'Brien wrote a grant and won $96,000 to purchase solar panels for campus buildings. Mackintosh students convinced school administrators to use the money saved on electricity to fund a "Solar Scholarship." The US Department of Education honored Mackintosh Academy with an environmental award.

Do an energy scavenger hunt with your classmates to find ways your school can save power.

NO WORLD TOO BiG

A golden shovel poem by **Keila V. Dawson**

Is there another Mother Earth? A Planet B? **No,**
this blue-and-green swirl—our only **world—**
deserves respect and protection, **too.**
Trapped heat. Melting ice. **Big**
storms rise, but **young**
activists are flooding with ideas. **People**
are awakening to the challenge and **fighting,**
working together and taking **global**
action. To heal a hurting **climate:**
Invent! Rethink! And speak up for **change!**

Like Greta Thunberg, you may feel angry at adults for knowing about climate change and not doing enough to try to fix it. You may feel anxious about the future or overwhelmed by the problem. However you feel, kids around the world share your emotions.

Climate change is a big problem. But no world is too big for you to do something about it.

FROM ME . . .

What can I do?

Most of the activists in this book started out making little changes at home or at school. Maya upcycled old clothes for herself, students at the Green School started carpooling, and Nikita and Sofiia-Khrystyna composted.

You are only one person, but you can make simple changes right now to reduce your climate impact.

- **Save water.** It takes a lot of energy to purify and heat the water that comes into our homes, so take a short shower instead of a bath.

- **Eat green.** Of all the things you eat, red meat has the biggest climate impact. Choose chicken or veggies more often, and don't waste food.

- **Save fuel.** Take the bus, carpool, ride a bike, or walk to school to reduce your climate impact.

- **Trap carbon.** Help reduce Earth's blanket of heat-trapping gases. Plant a tree or start a compost bin.

TO WE . . .

What can we do?

Zanagee wasn't able to reduce his school's single-use water bottle habit until he teamed up with friends. Greta joined youth all over the world to raise more voices for change.

When people move from "me" to "we," actions have greater impact—and everyone has more fun! You can work together with different groups.

- **Family:** Is it possible to switch your family's home to solar or wind power? If not, why not? Write to your power company and elected officials and ask for green energy.

- **School:** Scale up! If an average-sized elementary school had Meatless Mondays for a year, it could save twenty-two tons of greenhouse gas emissions.

- **Town:** Work to make walking and biking safer and easier. Contact your city officials to ask for improved sidewalks and crosswalks, new bike paths, or a "walking school bus" program.

- **Country and world:** Get loud! Join a youth climate organization to work for global change.

GLOSSARY

Activist: A person who takes committed action to solve a problem.

Biodiesel: A plant-based substitute for fossil-fuel diesel. Biodiesel is often made from used cooking oil.

Climate change: Long-term change in average weather patterns driven by the human release of greenhouse gases. These gases have caused Earth to heat more than 2 degrees Fahrenheit (1.1 degrees Celsius) since 1900.

Climate footprint: An estimate of the greenhouse gas emissions caused by the activities of a person, household, or company during a given period of time.

Climate justice: Climate solutions that take into account social inequities (see *equity*).

Climate neutrality: Balance of greenhouse-gas emissions with their removal from the air.

Ecosystem: The plants, animals, and other organisms living together in a given area, interacting with one another and the surroundings.

Equity: Making sure everyone has what they need to succeed; fairness. Inequity means the opposite of equity.

Fossil fuels: Energy sources that have limited supply: coal, oil, and natural gas. They are called fossil fuels because they are made from ancient, decomposed life.

Greenhouse effect: The process by which certain gases in Earth's atmosphere act like a blanket holding in heat energy from the sun. In the same way, a glass greenhouse or a car with the windows rolled up on a sunny day can trap and build up heat.

Greenhouse gases: Heat-trapping gases such as carbon dioxide, methane, and nitrous oxide.

Greenhouse gas emissions: The amount of heat-trapping gases that are released into Earth's atmosphere.

Sustainability: The ability to maintain something or keep it going without depleting or destroying resources.

Upcycling: Reusing an object by turning it into something better.

VISUALIZING GREENHOUSE GASES

Climate science is so complex that counting pounds or tons of greenhouse gases is not a perfect measurement of human impact on our global climate. But without something better, it is the standard way scientists estimate individual climate footprints.

Acrostic: A poem that spells a word or phrase with the first letter of each line.

Dansa: A poem that begins with a quintain (five-line stanza) and uses the opening line as the last line in every stanza. All other stanzas are quatrains (four lines) with a bbaA rhyme scheme.

Definition poem: A poem that describes the meaning of a word.

Dokugin renga: Renga is a Japanese form of linked verse written by multiple poets. Dokugin renga is written by one person. A renga contains a stanza pattern beginning with haiku (five syllables in the first and third lines and seven syllables in the second line), followed by a stanza of two lines with seven syllables each.

Dramatic monologue: A poem meant to be acted in which one character speaks to another.

Found poem: A poem created by taking words or phrases from another source and creating new meaning without plagiarizing the original text.

Free verse: This unrestricted style does not need to rhyme or follow a beat pattern.

Golden shovel: A poem form created by Terrance Hayes that borrows a line or phrase from a poem or quote and uses those words as the last word of each line.

Lục bát poem: A Vietnamese poetic form with alternating lines of six and eight syllables. Each pair of lines rhymes on the sixth syllable, and the eighth syllable of the second line provides a new rhyme for the next two lines.

Projective verse: A type of free verse in which line breaks, punctuation, and spacing inform the reader where to speed up, slow down, and pause. The poem's arrangement loosely reflects the subject matter.

Sea chantey: A modern poetic form based on call-and-response songs used as early as the sixteenth century on sailing ships. A chanteyman would sing a verse followed by a response from sailors as they performed physical labor while at sea.

One pound of carbon dioxide would fill 62 gallon milk jugs.

One metric ton (2,200 pounds) of carbon dioxide would fill a 1,400-square-foot house.

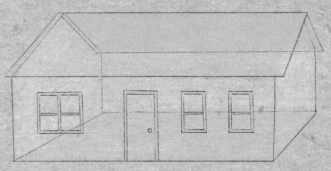

ABOUT THE POETS

David Bowles is an award-winning author and translator. Like Xiuhtezcatl Martinez, he is also a musician and an activist as one of the cofounders of #DignidadLiteraria, which fights for better Latinx representation in publishing. **davidbowles.us**

Jeanette Bradley once worked for fair-housing organizations, but now she writes and draws for kids. Her books include *Something Great; No Voice Too Small: Fourteen Young Americans Making History; Love, Mama;* and *When the Babies Came to Stay.* Jeanette lives in Rhode Island with her wife and kids. **jeanettebradley.com**

Vanessa Brantley-Newton is the author and illustrator of *Grandma's Purse* and *Just Like Me* and has illustrated many children's books. She studied fashion illustration at the Fashion Institute of Technology and children's book illustration at the School of Visual Arts in New York. Vanessa makes her nest in Charlotte, North Carolina. **vanessabrantleynewton.com**

JaNay Brown-Wood is an award-winning author and educator whose books have received starred reviews. Her debut, *Imani's Moon,* was featured on *The Late Show with Stephen Colbert* and *Storytime with The Met.* She enjoys writing and discussing the importance of authentic diversity in children's literature. **janaybrownwood.com**

Keila V. Dawson is a New Orleans native, former community organizer, and a coeditor of *No Voice Too Small.* She is the author of *Opening the Road: Victor Hugo Green and His Green Book* and *The King Cake Baby.* As an educator, she works with youth around the world to protect Planet Earth. **keiladawson.com**

Dalia Elhassan is a Sudanese American poet and writer based in New York City. She is the author of *In Half Light,* a chapbook in the New-Generation African Poets series. She is the recipient of the Hajja Razia Sharif Sheikh Prize in nonfiction and was short-listed for the 2018 Brunel International African Poetry Prize. **daliaelhassan.com**

Rajani LaRocca was born in India, raised in Kentucky, and now lives in the Boston area, where she practices medicine and writes award-winning novels and picture books. Like Maanasa Mendu, she finds inspiration in her family, her childhood, the natural world, math, science, and just about everything. **rajanilarocca.com**

Renée M. LaTulippe is the author of *The Crab Ballet* and *Limelight: Theater Poems to Perform* and has poems in many anthologies. She has experience in the performing arts, acting and directing, and is the founder of The Lyrical Language Lab and the Peek & Critique YouTube channel. **reneelatulippe.com**

Lindsay H. Metcalf is a journalist and award-winning author of nonfiction picture books, including *No Voice Too Small* and *Farmers Unite!* Lindsay lives in Kansas, not far from the farm where she grew up playing in the soil like Nikita Shulga and Sofiia-Khrystyna Borysiuk. **lindsayhmetcalf.com**

Aka Niviâna was born above the Arctic Circle in a small town in Northern Greenland and now lives in the capital, Nuuk. An activist and poet, Aka believes a complex series of social and environmental difficulties face the youth of Greenland. She advocates for the rights of Indigenous peoples.

Sally J. Pla is the award-winning author of books like *The Someday Birds* and cofounder of anovelmind.com, which explores neurodiversity and mental health in children's literature. Her eco-activism started in 1996 when she found a bird killed by pesticides on her lawn. Like Greta Thunberg, she's autistic. **sallyjpla.com**

Teresa Robeson is the author of *Queen of Physics*, which won the Asian/Pacific American Librarians Association Picture Book Award and was an International Literacy Association Primary Nonfiction Honor Book. As a decades-long environmental activist from Southeast Asia, Teresa applauds the green-fuel bus initiative in Bali. **teresarobeson.com**

Traci Sorell is an award-winning children's author of nonfiction and fiction, including *We Are Grateful: Otsaliheliga* and *We Are Still Here!* She is an enrolled citizen of the Cherokee Nation and lives in northeastern Oklahoma. Like Artemisa Xakriabá, Traci has advocated for Indigenous peoples to the US Congress. **tracisorell.com**

Heidi E. Y. Stemple is a National Science Teachers Association Outstanding STEM author who believes in the power of kids and science. Many of her books are about nature. She has made it her mission to teach as many children as she can to call owls—one school visit at a time. **heidieystemple.com**

Carlon Zackhras shares poetry about the Marshallese experience on Twitter. He became a climate activist at the first Youth Leadership Coalition: Combating Climate Change summit and helped facilitate a second summit that included dialogue with local leaders in the Marshall Islands. Carlon is currently pursuing a college degree.

Science Consultant

Stephen Porder is a professor of ecology and evolutionary biology at Brown University. He researches tropical forests and what happens when they are cleared for farmland. As Brown's assistant provost for sustainability, he focuses on ending the college's use of fossil fuels and transitioning to renewable energy.

For our shared future—J. B.

For all the eco-warriors everywhere—K. V. D.

For the matriarchs who continue to teach me: Mom, Kathy, and Mother Earth—L. H. M.

In an effort to offset the climate footprint of publishing and distributing this book, the editors are purchasing United Nations Certified Emission Reductions in the amount of ten pounds of greenhouse gas emissions per book sold.

Published by Charlesbridge
9 Galen Street
Watertown, MA 02472
(617) 926-0329
www.charlesbridge.com

Library of Congress Cataloging-in-Publication Data
Names: Metcalf, Lindsay H., editor. | Dawson, Keila V., editor. | Bradley, Jeanette, editor, illustrator.
Title: No world too big: young people fighting global climate change / edited by Lindsay H. Metcalf, Keila V. Dawson, and Jeanette Bradley; illustrated by Jeanette Bradley.
Description: Watertown: Charlesbridge Publishing, [2023] | Audience: Ages 5–9 | Audience: Grades 2–3 | Summary: "David Bowles, Traci Sorell, and others present poems about young activists who speak up to fight global climate change."—Provided by publisher.
Identifiers: LCCN 2021053654 (print) | LCCN 2021053655 (ebook) | ISBN 9781623543136 (hardcover) | ISBN 9781632899644 (ebook)
Subjects: LCSH: Social action—Juvenile poetry. | Climatic changes—Juvenile poetry. | Children's poetry, American. | CYAC: Social action—Poetry. | Climatic changes—Poetry. | American poetry. | LCGFT: Poetry.
Classification: LCC PS595.S75 N65 2023 (print) | LCC PS595.S75 (ebook) | DDC 811/.608—dc23/eng/20211116
LC record available at https://lccn.loc.gov/2021053654
LC ebook record available at https://lccn.loc.gov/2021053655

Printed in China
(hc) 10 9 8 7 6 5 4 3 2 1

Illustrations painted digitally in Procreate for iPad on a digital paper design by Paper Farms
Display type set in Brush Up by PintassilgoPrints
Text type set in Grenadine MVB by Markanna Studios Inc.
Printed by 1010 Printing International Limited in Huizhou, Guangdong, China
Production supervision by Nicole Turner
Designed by Diane M. Earley

NIKITA SHULGA AND
SOFiiA-KHRYSTYNA BORYSIUK
UKRAiNE

LEAH NAMUGERWA
UGANDA

GREEN SCHOOL
INDONESiA